A

WORD

Fitly Spoken

is like apples of gold in a setting of silver.

Proverbs 25:11

Messages from the Holy Spirit

Dr. Charles L. Kent

Published in the United States of America
ISBN: 978-0-578-65860-5

For information and inquiries:

Email: admin@awordfitlyspoken.net

Website: www.awordfitlyspoken.net

Facebook: A Word Fitly Spoken with Dr Charles Kent

You Tube: A Word Fitly Spoken

DEDICATIONS

I want to thank GOD for His goodness to me, and for this wonderful gift that He has bestowed upon me. I would like to dedicate this book to the fathers in my life, the men that made me who I am today. First my biological father Leroy Kent, a minister, a civil rights leader and entrepreneur, a real father. Thank you, Sir, for teaching me in my early years of development.

Then there was Elder Andrew Davis, my mentor at Morgan Park Assembly church in Chicago, Illinois. When I came to meet him, I was a real wreck. He taught me how to pray, how to study, and how to teach GOD's word. The time I was with him my foundation in Christ was solidified. Thank you, Sir, "I will catch up with you later and my natural father in heaven".

Finally, my current father in the faith, Dr. Garnet M. Budge a man of God, who has been my mentor for the last 20 plus years; he has opened up the scriptures to me concerning the Apostolic Restoration Movement and opened my eyes to the international scope of ministry on my life. He's the one who introduced me to Australia as well as Africa, where I have traveled over a dozen times. He also taught me so much about flowing in the supernatural.

Jesus said to His disciples, in St. John 14:12, "Son's greater works than what I've done shall you do, because I go to my father." Greater didn't come upon these men until their father went to his father. I honor these great men of GOD who continued to go to their father and to show me the way. This is part of my way of saying Thank You.

Dr. Charles Kent

ACKNOWLEDGEMENT

I want to first recognize my family and friends and their support. Especially my beautiful wife and how encouraging you have been as it relates to this gift.

"I thank God that I finally found someone."
Love you Juleane.

Special recognition goes Rena A. Hillery and Dr. Melanie P. Manor, these two played a very important role in the actual production of this work, and for that I say thank you.

Some time ago, one of my daughters in the faith came to me and said, "Pastor I have over 30 of your acronyms and I have only been here for a couple of years. I know you have more than that. You should write a book." Rena stayed persistent about writing this book. She located a publishing company and assisted in a lot of the typing. Thanks Rena, for your inspiration.

I would like to recognize all my friends worldwide, who have yet to walk in their destiny, understand their gifts, and experience what it's like to know you gave it all. To you, I say, "don't bury that gift, and find a way to get it out there. When you do, you'll be pleased, others will be grateful, and you'll sense God's smile of approval over your life."

To my flocks that have supported me in this journey from Australia, Africa and the USA, your eagerness to listen and to learn has caused these acronyms to grow in me. Thank you for being part of God's training ground.

TABLE OF CONTENTS

FOREWORD

When Dr. Charles Kent told me that he was going to publish his book with his world-famous acronyms, it was all I could do to keep from shouting aloud. *"Sure, Dr. Kent"*, I said. I tried to encourage him before, but he never made a move toward it. Inwardly, I knew once he started, he would run through the process with *fire*. I have read these acronyms, and I see how he meshes them into his teaching. I knew once he began this, the acronyms would bless the world; I have even used some of them in my teaching.

Dr. Kent is a master teacher to me, his passion bursts when he is in his element. Dr. Kent lives, breathes, and eats in the world of acronyms. Over the last few years, as Dr. Kent methodically worked his way through this first set of inspiring acronyms, I began to wonder if he could ever stop and get it done since he traveled so much to do the work of the Lord. Each time I spoke to him, he was somewhere other than the states. When he wasn't sitting at his desk at church or assisting nations abroad, he was discussing how these acronyms could change the minds of people. He was prowling the skyways of the nation's advancing Joseph Outreach Ministries in Australia, and Africa, trying to begin this wonderful piece that's so rich. He was always on the go; I often asked myself, does this man ever sleep?

To the casual reader, this book will be impressive because of its sheer size, but practitioners of local and regional history will be astonished by the book's depth of detail, spiritual jolts, and complexity.

Finally, Dr. Kent has put together acronyms which bring back personal reflection of life's sometimes unpleasant memories, but this allows you to not tread those waters in the same state ever again. This is a remarkable book, a study guide, an inspirational blast for your soul all rolled into one. It is a double-edged sword for the user. From all of us who continued to doubt and not utilize the **GIFT** (God's Instrument For Transformation) that GOD gave us, thank you, Dr. Kent for being a pioneer among us who are still sitting on our gift.

Dr. Melanie P. Manor
Aspiring Knowledge, Inc. - CVO

INTRODUCTION

As a new believer in Christ Jesus, I overheard someone speaking about "the *perfect* will of God". I was so amazed that God had a *perfect* will for my life. It was then I discovered my gift of teaching. I begin a lifelong search for knowledge, insight, and wisdom.

I came across so much truth and remember asking God to help me to retain the thoughts that He was directly downloading to me. I was truly enlightened by His word and His spirit. God gave me this gift of remembering events, scripture lessons, teaching tools, and defining special moments through acronyms, hence the title, "A WORD FITLY SPOKEN".

It's nothing short of a miracle. I give Him all the Glory! For years I've ministered using one, two, and even more of my acronyms in my teachings. These acronyms help put a handle on the truths discovered as we look into life and the word of God.
The way God deals with me is through meditation, and I simply ask Him, "What are you saying? How could this be said in a way that will allow me to never forget? Give me a method, to hunt this truth on", and as expected, He does it each time.

So, I invite you to walk with me through these life lessons using the acronyms given to me by God, that reveal to us how to handle His precious principles which He desires us to never forget.

ABRAM

Now the Lord said to Abram, get out of your country, from your family, and from your father's house. To a land that I will show you, I will make you a great nation; I will bless you and make your name great; and you shall be a blessing.

Scripture: Genesis 12

A
Big
Revelation
About
Money

What a defining moment in this man's life, a word from GOD, was the start of making Abram the *"Father of Faith"*. The next few things that took place in his life would define him for the rest of his life. Promises from GOD to Abram required some things for him to do, in order for him to take possession of these precious promises. I sometimes wondered if he stayed home, would his name have become great. If he did not leave his father's house, would he have not seen the Promised Land? So much of the manifestations of the promises of GOD are wrapped up even sometimes hidden in our obedience. Leaving family, leaving friends, and leaving our familiar circumstances, got GOD's attention.

Abram was very rich in livestock, in silver, and gold. The faith that this man exhibited put him on a path to greatness. He dared to step out and move on with what GOD told him to do. And as a result, GOD blessed him abundantly. He had plenty of money and it was all about Abram's obedience that caused him to be blessed.

GOD demonstrated that it was "A Big Revelation About Money" in the life of this man of faith.

AFRAID

If you have faith, fear will sap it out of you if you allow it to. The devil is waiting on you. When you are vulnerable, he comes in to steal, kill and destroy. We are in fear because the enemy does not announce that he is coming; he comes secretly.

Scripture: Mark 4: 35-41; St. John 6:16-24

The enemy comes to attack your faith, with **A F**aith **RAID**. We need to recognize when we are under attack and guard our faith and not be afraid. Being Afraid can be:

Another

Fact (that's)

Really

Advantageous

In

Decisions

Why Be Afraid? GOD has a pattern of showing up in the midst of your storm, if you will have an eye to see HIM. He will manifest Himself to you. In the midst of your problems, look to Jesus, the author and finisher of your faith.

II Timothy 1:7 states,

"GOD has not given us the spirit of fear, but of power, love and a sound mind."

AGREE

The word, agree is not the word we use to describe unison, no but rather the English word we use to describe harmony.

Matthew 18:19 states: *"Again I say to you that if two of you agree on earth concerning anything that they ask, it will be done for them."*

The understanding is to bring about harmony. Our acronym lends itself to an aggressive move to get rid of the rational reasons why we don't harmonize, i.e., work together.

Scripture: Amos 3:3: Matthew 18:19

If we are a part of a jazz band; someone must be the bandmaster and determine who's too loud, who's too soft, and when the saxophone does its solo etc. GOD is the leader He calls those shots, but we play the instruments.

It is so easy to think and even demand that everybody around you and I should be like we are. Wear the same things; think the same way, even like the same foods. GOD made every star and every snowflake different, yet they work together with all their differences. GOD made man and woman differently and yet He says agree; to see the same thing is to see harmony at the end of the song, one beautiful sound. My suggestion is stop with the excuses of why we can't agree with each other, sing our part, play our instrument, and the maestro will smile when we're all finished. AGREE!

Aggressively

Getting

Rid (of)

Every

Excuse

BARREN

Before GOD does a thing, He will announce it through His prophets. It's very important to have an ear to hear what the spirit of GOD is saying as well as what GOD plans to do.

Scripture: Luke 1:7-12

My brothers and sisters, what is GOD up to with you and your walk with Him, with you and your family, with you and your church family? The point is "*Jesus is coming soon*" and there's a particular pattern He chooses to use as a launching pad for His entrance into earth. Let's take a look:

Elizabeth and Zacharias were GOD's least likely choice as forerunners because they were old, and he was silenced until the manifestation because of his disobedience.

Zacharias was doing his duties in the temple and there appeared an angel of the Lord. A dramatic, awesome, memorable event like a Damascus Road Experience: GOD has to interrupt our regular course with something supernatural and He will. When Zacharias saw the angel, he was troubled, and fear fell upon him. Elizabeth was barren but favored by GOD to carry the forerunner for Christ. Barren is:

Breaking

All

Religious

Rules (and)

Ending

Negativity

No one can make you feel inferior without your consent --
Eleanor Roosevelt

BEST

In order to get better, we need to do our best by doing away with the former thoughts.

Scripture: Daniel 5:11-12, Romans 12:2, Numbers 14:24

An old person told me one day *"Good Better Best, Good Better Best, Never, Never Rest, until your good is better and your better is best"*. Our best is what we do not once in a while; but rather it's an attitude, a disposition, and a mindset. Doing our best is being excellent even when no one is looking. We sense the victory and know if I just give my best, victory is certain.

I have had many instructors that structured things in me, because they demanded my best. Dr. Bennie Goodwin stands out. I befriended Dr. Bennie Goodwin and thought I could just dazzle him with my writing style. I waited until the last minute to write my term paper. No rough drafts, no editing, no proofreading. I got a failing score on that paper. I had never seen so much red ink in all my life. His words at the end of the paper changed my life forever. He stated, *"It's a shame, such strong content is so poorly constructed, DO IT OVER!!!"* Trust me, It has never been forgotten.

Our best is:

Being
    Excellent (and)
   Seeing
    Triumph

There's only one corner of the universe you can be certain of improving, and that's your own self. --Aldous Huxley

BETTER

The biggest room in the house is the room for improvement.
The theme of the book of Hebrews is better *(A Better Way)*.

Scriptures: Hebrews 1:4, Hebrew 8:6

Better covenant established upon better promises. Sometimes
it is difficult for us to understand when we are getting better.
Better things come to people who are mature. When we
become mature, we will:

Believe

Every

Test (and)

Trial

Ends

Right

We can't get better if we are bitter. There are some things
we need to get better in so that we don't become bitter. We
need to better our:

- Prayer life.
- Prophesies. Words have spirit and life. Have
  prophetic words, a prophetic voice.
- Walk with GOD
- Praise and worship.
  *How is your praise when things are not going
  well?*
- Preaching places and platforms
- Best presentation unto people

BLIND

Blind from birth, living in darkness, a birth defect. Blind means the inability to see clearly, possibly an abnormality in the womb, a deficiency.

Scripture: John 9:2

Basically

Living

In

Need

Daily

The solutions to living in need on a daily basis, is found here in this text. Jesus spat on the ground and made clay and anointed the man's eyes with the clay and then told him to go and wash in the pool of Siloam. So he went, washed, and came back seeing. Here lies a principle for meeting needs, not only physical needs, but supernatural needs. Jesus takes a part of Himself, His saliva and mixes it with something natural, i.e., the clay from the earth and then places that combination on the problem area.

Whenever we have a situation of blindness, get a word from GOD, and take it into your natural mind and watch a supernatural manifestation of GOD take place.

BOAT

Jonah got in a boat going in the wrong direction. He paid money to board this boat. He was comfortable in his decision. When we make a decision to do something contrary to what GOD has said, then we pay the price for it. *How many of us are paying to go in the wrong direction?*

Because of Jonah's presence on that boat a disturbance was caused in the sea. Due to Jonah's disobedience the lives of everyone on the boat was in jeopardy.

Scripture: Jonah 1

Sometimes our decision to go in the wrong direction affects more than just ourselves. *Who are you affecting with your decisions?*

Going in the wrong direction is:

Big

Opportunities (that)

Aren't

Truth

Many opportunities come our way, but are they of GOD? Are they the direction that GOD would have us to go?

BOSS

The protocol of faith is about order, the proper way of doing a thing. The lack of protocol will get you in trouble. We must be pleasing to the sight of GOD. The way to do this is by having faith.

Scripture: Hebrew 11:6

By faith things happen. Faith is the BOSS of the universe. The things of GOD have protocol, and faith has protocol. The ingredients for the protocol of Faith are BOSS:

Believing (work on what you believe)

Obeying (this is crucial)

Speaking (and)

Seeing (see things with a supernatural eye)

Without faith, it's impossible to please Him. The protocol, procedure, principle, policy, and pattern of faith are all about how this idea works; the necessary steps have not changed over the years. Back in the day, I spent time in the kitchen, I enjoyed baking pies. One of my favorite was strawberry cream cheese, and I would do it with a graham cracker crust. I remember not having all of my ingredients and still trying to make it work.

It didn't work, and some people were kind enough to tell me, *"There's just something missing here"*. And others were not so nice and said, *"What happened, Charles, this isn't your best"*. No matter how it's relayed to you, if you're missing one of these ingredients as it relates to faith, it will be incomplete. *Believe! Obey! Speak! and See!* - it takes them all to produce a productive faith-walk.

BUSY

Being busy doesn't mean we're effective. Much of what we do can be labeled as errands that erode effectiveness. If you don't know where you're going any road will take you there. There will always be someone that will tell you what you should be doing as long as you allow them.

Scripture: Romans 8:14; Isaiah 30:15; Matthew 11:28-29

Romans 8:14 says, *"For as many as are led by the Spirit are the Sons of **GOD**.*

Do you get in the car and immediately turn the music up? When I was not a Christian the music came on as soon as my hands left the keys, the enemy's assignment was to keep my *M.I.N.D, the Main Ingredient Navigating Destiny,* busy. Wait a minute slow down here. *"In quietness and confidence will be your strength."* **Isaiah 30:15**

Have you felt that things have just gotten a little bit too heavy, the hustle and the coming and going. Many times, we can barely remember where we were the last hour. In the technology age of cell phones, I-Pads, Bluetooth, and computers, *when do we have any time for GOD?* I'm so glad I'm considered "Old School", that means I understand technology is here and here to stay. I just know how to shut it off when I need to. One writer said, "GOD was not in the storm, nor in the loud voice, but rather in a still small voice." We're just a little too B.U.S.Y.

Being

Under

Satan's

Yoke

CARE

This is one of the very first acronyms GOD gave me.

Before there was a church, an international ministry, and even one trip to Africa, there was a sound from heaven. I heard in my ear a word from GOD to demonstrate real CARE everywhere. So, I started WE C.A.R.E. Ministries. It took on a life of its own, how do we reach everyone with the message of Jesus Christ? GOD began to show me ways and means of accomplishing this. *"Go ye into all the world was the beginning and make disciples."* **Matthew 28:19.**

Scripture: Matthew 28:19; II Samuel 7:7 My ministry was established on this platform **C.A.R.E.**

Concerned

About

Reaching

Everybody

In **II Samuel 7:7**; David desires to build a house for GOD; a noble and good idea. "I live", David says, in a house of Cedar, but the ark of GOD dwelleth within curtains. GOD's response to David's idea and dream was what GOD showed me many years ago. Let us look at this scripture as GOD spoke to David.

*"In all the places wherein I have walked; with all the children of Israel spoke a word with any of the tribes of Israel, **whom I commanded to feed my people** Israel, saying why build ye not me a house of cedar."* It appears to me GOD was more concerned about leaders feeding than building buildings. Caring more than construction; building up people more so than building buildings.

I've spent my life building people, feeding people, and caring!!

Man is a creature who lives not upon bread alone, but principally by catch words --Robert Louis Stevenson

CAVE

Scripture: I Samuel 22:1-2

Can you imagine this situation David wants to just get away from it all? He finds a CAVE to hide in, but he must drive out the previous tenants, wild animals, snakes, and bears. Nobody wants to live in a cave. David thinks nobody will find him there, but when people recognize the anointing on your life, they'll come to you no matter where you are and what you're going through personally.

David escapes to the Cave of Adullam, so when his brothers and his entire father's house heard it, they came to him. Everyone who was in distress, in debt, was discontented gathered to him. So, he became captain over them and there were about 400 men with him. When people are meant to be with you a cold, dark, dreary, animal infested environment will not keep them away. The word got out, *"where's David?"* He's in a CAVE, notice what they don't say, like "W*hy is he there?*" they just say, "I'm out of here, I'm going where my leader is. I'm connected, he has what I need to breathe, what I need to survive and thrive." 400 men end up joining David in this:

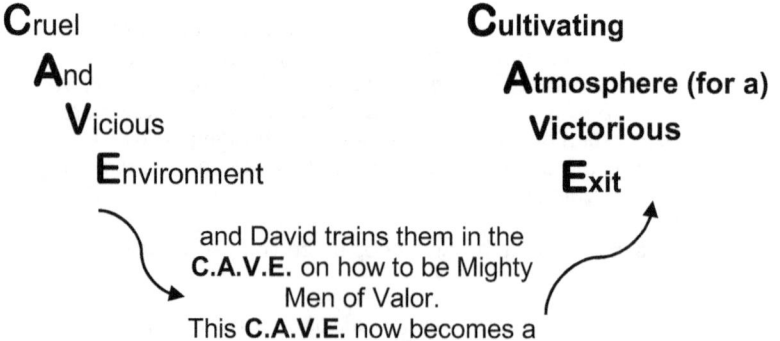

Cruel   **C**ultivating

     And   **A**tmosphere (for a)

       Vicious   **V**ictorious

         Environment   **E**xit

and David trains them in the **C.A.V.E.** on how to be Mighty Men of Valor. This **C.A.V.E.** now becomes a

*Which **C.A.V.E** are you in?*

20

COACH

There have been many great teams and great individual sports figures. But in all cases, there's somebody behind the scenes, motivating, challenging, and seeing more than even that person in the ring. An Author once quoted, *"It's a shame when someone else sees more in you than you see in yourself."* This is a person that's willing to show you who you really are and is willing to take your abuse and reluctance in pursuing your dreams. That person is known as **COACH**.

Cultivating

Optimism

And

Conquering

Hypocrisy

Allow me to explain, in the book of Esther there's a man of God named Mordecai who is sent to cultivate optimism in young Esther, but not just cultivate optimism through Mordecai's coaching but also to conquer Esther's hypocritical attitude that says, "I can't there's, just no way." Coaches do and see what many others don't see as Mordecai did.

Scripture: Esther 2

They can handle our disappointments in our ability, and frustrations when we didn't get it right and had to do it over again. It takes a special person to be called to come along side and motivate another to places and plateaus they've never experienced before. "*C.O.A.C.H: Cultivating Optimism And Conquering Hypocrisy*". We all need one, and in a lot of cases we need to become a *coach* to some up and coming champion.

Learning teacheth more in one year than experience in twenty.
--Roger Ascham

DOORS

When you consistently knock, doors are supposed to open, if we are not experiencing open heavens, then there is something wrong.

Peter was therefore kept in prison, but constant prayer was offered to GOD for him by the Church…

Scripture: Acts 12:5-17; Psalms 78:23

- Verse 7 says, *"Now behold an angel of the Lord stood by him, and a light shined in the prison: and he struck Peter on the side and raised him up, saying "Arise quickly" and his chains fell off his hands…"*

- Verse 10 says, *"When they were past the first and second guard posts, they came to the Iron Gate that leads to the city, which opened to them on its own accord."*

Doors are only manifested when coupled with obedience. *What is a door?* A door is a:

Distinct

Obedient

Opportunity

Rarely

Seen

Intelligence is quickness to apprehend as distinct from ability, which is capacity to act wisely on the thing apprehended. -- Alfred North Whitehead

DREAMS

Hope deferred makes the heart sick. It's time to resurrect our hope.

Scripture: Genesis 37

Daring (to)

Reach

Every

Available

Mindset

Supernaturally

Steps to the fulfillment of your dreams:

- **Parental Preference**--You need your parents or somebody to speak over you. Parents have powerful words to speak into their children's lives. Be careful about your parental preference.
- **Prophetic Pronouncement**-- A word spoken over your life from GOD.
- **People**— You have got to have people that come against you to prove your point, which challenges the word that is in your spirit.
- **Problems**—Are going to come, they produce power. If you don't have any problems, you will not draw near to GOD.
- **Preview of Promotion**—In the midst of your problems GOD will always give you a preview of your promotion. Previews in the pursuit of your dreams bring peace. A preview is a sample of what GOD wants to do in your life.
- **Promotion**- There will be plenty and there will be pain. There is a plateau that GOD will take you and other people just cannot go.

All men dream; but not equally, those who dream by night in the dusty recesses of their minds wake in the day to find that it was vanity: but the dreamers of the day are dangerous men, for they may act their dreams with open eyes, to make it possible. --T.E. Lawrence

ENEMY

Moses said to the people, *"Do not be afraid, stand still and see the salvation of the Lord, which He will accomplish for you today. For the Egyptians whom you see today, you shall see again no more forever"*.

Scripture: Exodus 14:13, 1 Cor. 15:25-26

For He must reign till He has put all enemies under His feet, the last enemy that will be destroyed is death.
An Enemy is:

Every

    Nemesis

        Entering

           My

              Yard

In the Old Testament, the Egyptians were the enemies of the children of Israel, slave masters, who kept them in bondage for over 400 years. A *Cruel And Vicious Environment* (C.A.V.E) was what they lived in every single day. They remind me of "bullies" like those I was growing up with on the streets of Chicago, Illinois. Most enemies are territorial, they have certain regions or neighborhoods that they terrorize, and they don't tend to venture too far beyond that area.

Occasionally you will find an enemy, who wants to increase his territory, who wants to advance his area of influence and steps into my Y.A.R.D- Your Area of Responsibility and Destiny. There's nothing that made me more upset than to have an enemy in my yard talking noise. The children of Israel are out of Egypt no longer under the control of Pharaoh and his evil ways. When Israel gets to their territory, the red sea, "*they turn around*", and saw their old nemesis, the Egyptians and GOD is angered. I can hear GOD say, "*Not in my backyard, not on my turf*". We ought to tell sickness, disease, poverty, and death, *"not in my yard"*!

FAITH

Abraham is known as the Father of Faith. Many people have been branded by acts of bravery or defining moments. Such is the case with this mighty man, the father of many nations. It's in this statement of faith to the young men standing by watching and knowing what it'll take to get this job done. I believe they said to themselves, "*Has the old man lost it, does he not know he needs a lamb to complete this sacrifice*".

He's not thinking too clearly, should we mention it to him? He doesn't have everything he needs for this assignment to get done. Abraham moves in an assurance many of us only dream about. Things don't have to be clearly spelled out to him. Abraham is accustomed to GOD leading him to step out on faith and to have full assurance in his heart. Years earlier he left his family with only a sound from heaven, i.e., a Word from GOD.

Faith Is:

Full

Assurance

In

The

Heart

Scripture: Genesis 22:5, 7-8

Abraham seems to be able to trust GOD when he can't trace him. "*I and the lad will go and return*". Was he going to offer his son or not? The rest of the story indicates he had every intent and belief that somehow GOD would raise up his son. **Hebrews 11:6** *says,"...without faith it's impossible to please Him, for he who comes to GOD must believe that He is, and that He is a rewarder of those who diligently seek Him."*

FATHER

"May the Lord GOD of your fathers' make you a thousand times more numerous than you are and bless you as He has promised you!"

Scripture: Deuteronomy 1:11

A Father is a:

Faithful

Authority

That

Has

Every

Right

Our father GOD, and the promises made, make all the difference in your life today. Good fathers that have real good relationship with GOD request, strike deals, and negotiate on behalf of their children and grandchildren. It's a father's determination that brings a blessing to the offspring; this has been proven throughout time.

David made a covenant with Jonathan. Jonathan requested, *"Save my household after I'm dead and gone"*, and David honored his word. GOD is the GOD of Abraham, Isaac, and Jacob. Generational blessings are what we see here. Many of the riches that we enjoy are because our forefathers requested them for us, in the natural as well as in the spiritual. And it's because of that faithfulness, good fathers truly have every right to say what they feel as it relates to our development. We're their seed, they birthed us.

FAVOR

Many of us feel that favor comes to a person because of their looks, or by being born into a particular family or having friends of great influence. The idea of us working to achieve favor is far from many of us, but it is very much in the mind of GOD. Case in point: Joseph of the Old Testament. Over and over, it says, *"And GOD was with him"*. In prison, in a scandal with the bosses' wife, and in domestic disturbances, GOD was with him. The amazing thing is that Joseph was with GOD through it all. Much of what we go through, GOD is committed to being with you and me, it's just sometimes we ask the Holy Spirit to leave the room and let us handle this one "our way".

Scripture: Genesis 37-50

Favor Is:

Faithfulness

Appreciated

Violating

Obvious

Rules

Joseph was faithful to GOD in every case, consistent, steadfast no matter what. Doing what is right for right sake just because it's the right thing to do. Joseph said, "I will not sin before my GOD or my boss". GOD sees and appreciates your faithfulness and now He'll show you how much He appreciates you by violating obvious rules for you.

What a word, what favor from GOD! You know you don't deserve it. All of us know or at least question how they got it. Their faithfulness has been appreciated by GOD and GOD is violating obvious rules for them. *Favor Ain't Fair*!

FEAR

Two thirds of the word fear is ear, it's what we hear in our ear that brings about fear. The evidence is clear, the doctor's report is back, and it appears to be negative. The court has ruled, and the evidence says jail time is going to happen for your child.

Scripture: I Kings 19: 1-3

In our case study Elijah gets evidence in his ears you're going to die tomorrow about this same time. **F**orget **E**verything **A**nd **R**un is his only option. The evidence was clear, a messenger from Jezebel showed up. Running seemed to be the safest course of action, but just one thing was missing, a word from the Lord. *Is there not a word from the Lord in these times?* Just as we turn our ear to hear the words of fear, maybe we ought to turn our ears to the words of faith, especially, after GOD gave Elijah such a great victory. The expectation and knowledge of the ability of GOD should have been very fresh in Elijah's memory, but he failed to re-member like most of us after GOD does something awesome in our lives. We're so quick to dis-member the thought of his most recent victory, and we forget it when an opportunity for fear creeps in.

F.E.A.R. is and can be:

False		**F**orget
Evidence		**E**verything
Appearing	**OR**	**A**nd
Real		**R**un

FIELD

The story of Ruth is a beautiful one--a dream come true. A rags to riches story that never gets old. This young, committed woman was dedicated to serving her elderly mother-in-law, Naomi.

To Ruth, Naomi demonstrated knowledge of the true GOD even though she had great losses and was very bitter. Ruth says to this bitter woman in the tough times "*bid me not to go away*". The tone was strong and emphatic because it states Naomi never again mentioned Ruth leaving her.

Scripture: Ruth 2:4-6

In Ruth chapter 2, Ruth meets up with Boaz, her future husband. It's very intriguing in the latter part of verse 3 it says, *"she happened to come to the part of the field belonging to Boaz"*. This was destiny but she didn't know it. While she was gleaning, she had stumbled upon a rich man's field--Boaz. She was gleaning behind the reapers like a slave girl and about to become the owner of the field.

A Field is a:

Fantastic

Instruction (and)

Entrance (to a)

Life (of)

Destiny

It was fantastic that Ruth was given instructions from Naomi. This was an entrance to her life of destiny. Where is your field? Much of what we stumble up on is a field GOD wants us to eventually own. Be careful not to overlook your GOD ordained field just because you think it is a mediocre or belittling task. For every one of us, we have a field, a Fantastic Instruction and Entrance to a Life of Destiny.

FOOL

A fool has said in his heart there is no GOD. The book of Proverbs is filled with action words. The compiling of these Proverbs is done in a contrast format. A fool is compared and put in contrast to a wise man. For example, he who walks with wise men will be wise, but the companion of fools will be destroyed.

Scripture: Proverbs 13:20

A Fool is:

Forsaking

Our

Original

Learning

How do we get to a point of becoming a fool or acting foolishly? I see it like this: in the beginning there was a garden where man and GOD communed every day. Then there came a day where man decided he no longer needed to keep his appointments with GOD. What a mistake! Foolish mistake! Man neglected to remember the original lessons taught to him by the Almighty.

We just don't come out of the womb disrespecting or not acknowledging GOD, it's a learned procedure, much like what happened in the Garden of Eden. Man forsook our original lessons of life, love, and loyalty to the Lord of Lords, the King of Kings. What a foolish thing to do.

GIFT

GOD gave gifts to man, some of the gift's GOD gave are Apostles, Pastors, Prophets, Evangelists, and Teachers. Gifts, talents, abilities, and charisma are attributes GOD has given you that come to you almost naturally. Having these attributes is rather challenging for someone else to do even after much education and training. Gifted, just plain gifted we call them, *how does she do that, and how does he make it look so easy?*

Scripture: Ephesians 4:7-8

We've seen the gifted actors, musicians, sport figures, and individuals. It seems the more I travel the more I recognize GOD's gift to man. Let me use Detroit, Michigan for example. When I was growing up, that was a city where it seemed so many "gifted" singers lived. GOD was just showing off! I felt it seemed a little unfair for so many great gifted singers to all come from one city. I believe the gift can be misused and even abused. In my travels to West Africa, I see so many diamonds. One day I sat and inspected over 8,000 carats of diamonds. In that region it's so plentiful, and it's nothing to find large diamonds in the backyard of the locals. These are gifts from GOD. I often wonder why GOD put diamonds, gold, emeralds, rubies, oil, and gas in the soil of Africa and the local people benefit the least from GOD's gifts.

A GIFT is:

God's

Instrument

For

Transformation

Whether you're a teacher, preacher, sports professional, writer, a mom, or a son, maybe you're just a diamond in the rough. Don't bury your gift. GOD gave it to be an instrument to bring about change and transformation supernaturally. My friend, at some point GOD will come back and ask: "**What did you do with the gift I gave you?**"

It is a great ability to be able to conceal one's ability   -
-La Rocheforecauld

GO FORWARD

The story seems to be too good to be true. The children of Israel are finally free; they're out of Egypt on their way to the land of promise. They were faced with mountains on both sides of them, a massive Red Sea in front of them, and let's not forget their former slave masters coming after them. Moses, the reluctant leader, is now in a real mess. What do you do when all around you people are complaining about your leadership abilities?

Scripture: Exodus 14:15

Verse 15 of Exodus, says, The Lord said to Moses, *"why do you cry to me?" Tell the children of Israel to go forward."*

What a statement for a people that had only known slavery for over 400 years, they're not leaders, not military minded warriors, and yet the instructions are clear from heaven. Hear what GOD meant by those words:

Get
    Optimistic

       Forsaking
      Our
        Routine (and)
         Willingly
          Anticipate
           Real
            Destiny

To all of us facing insurmountable odds, being surrounded by challenges we need to hear the word of the Lord and **GO FORWARD!!**

GREATER

At some time in our lives, we just have to decide that we can do more, a lot more than what we're doing now.

Scripture: John 14:12

The spirit of a real father always wants his offspring to go beyond what he accomplishes. We can believe what we may but, to do a true study of the word, let's look at the first time the word greater was introduced in scripture. **Genesis 1:16**; "*GOD made two great lights; the greater to rule by day and the lesser to rule by night*". Two great lights but one is greater than the other.

GOD says the sun is greater, therefore whenever GOD says; He's going to do something "greater", it's going to be as different as night is to day. No matter how sweet and beautiful the moonlight might be, the sun is greater. You and I have had some "great times, some great days, some great relationships", but there's something greater that is coming as different as night is to day and there is no comparison. **John 15:13** says, *"Greater love hath no man than this that a man lay down his life for a friend"*. There's love and then there's greater love.

Greater means to me:

Goodness

Revealed

Exceeding

All

The

Existing

Records

Greater is record breaking stuff, and remember as a Christian, Greater is He that is within you than He that is in the world. My friend there's *just (Nobody Greater)*! Thanks Dan from Forerunners Gold Coast, Australia, for your words of wisdom.

HOPE

So much of what motivates us and just keeps us going is hope. I was fortunate to have an elderly woman live in my home from the time she was 60 until she died at 77. She was blind most of her life and out lived four husbands and raised ten children. Granny came to stay with my wife and I shortly after we were married. She had a number of health problems aside from her sight, but she got up every morning with a song on her lips. She lived to help raise my children and to assist with all her grandchildren. Granny had a great hope to one day see Jesus Christ and no amount of daily pain could cloud her vision for heaven. I watched her get slower and slower physically, and stronger and stronger in her hope.

It seemed like the hope was the stabilizing force in her life, along with having something to do every day, i.e., dealing with Denise, Josh, and Charmaine. It gave her power to overcome any personal pain. She was old, blind, sickly, in a lot of pain, but yet, she remained full of hope until the very end.

Scripture: Hebrews 6:19

Granny you showed us all how to experience: Healing of Our Pain Every day and you definitely Helped Other People Excel.

Healing	**H**elping
Our	**O**ther
Pain	**P**eople
Everyday	**E**xcel

Thanks Dora!

Although the world is full of suffering, it is full also of the overcoming of it. --Helen Keller

34

LEFT

There will always be times of plenty and times of not so much. GOD has promised His people that He would never leave them, and so in the midst of difficult times expect GOD. When all is looking like you're surrounded, GO FORWARD. When all seems to be lost, look around for what you have left. GOD specializes in taking what's left and bringing greatness out of that situation.

Scripture: II Kings 4: 2-3

In Our case study, the woman says to the Prophet Elijah, in her desperation, "this is all that I have, and it appears my life is over after this". But GOD knew that He was about to establish a business through this situation. This was the right season for Elijah to come.

What she had left in her house was a:

Life (of)

Enterprising

Faith

Today

Naomi lost her home, husband, and sons, but what she had left was Ruth, that would bring about Boaz, Obed, Jesse, David, and eventually Jesus the Messiah.

GOD will always ask you about what you have left, not what you have lost. After everything is taken, what do you still have down inside of you? There is a destiny over your life and GOD will use what is left when you go through suffering and loss.

LIES

Scripture: Mark 11:23

"For assuredly, I say to you, whosever says to this mountain. Be removed and be cast into the sea, and does not doubt in his heart, but believes that those things he says will be done, he will have whatever he says."

While I was in Brussels, Belgium not too far from The Kings Palace and the Headquarters for the European Union GOD spoke to me. It was a beautiful place where the food was fabulous, the clothing shops were excellent, and I saw cars there I couldn't name. Wealth like I'd never seen before. As I walked the streets, I asked GOD these questions. "Is this what you want for your children? Is this what's going on in Heaven?

At that moment GOD spoke and said to me "Charles whatever you say. You shall have whatever you say". Then He said something else. GOD said, "You're my mouthpiece and I cannot lie, so when you say something out of your mouth, I've got to make it so. So, Charles please stop with the lies, and stop saying stuff I didn't say, it's a lie". Yes, it may be a logical interpretation, but it'll eat away or erode the supernatural. Let the poor say I'm rich, let the weak say I'm strong. It's whatever you say, and you and I need to stop with the lies, because a lie is a:

Logical

Interpretation (that)

Erodes (the)

Supernatural

LOST

The story of Ruth starts with a man bringing his wife and two sons to a country called Moab. The boys marry two Moabites women, Naomi husband dies, her two sons die and even one of Naomi's daughter in-laws leave. What a loss, we would think. Let us look further.

Scripture: Ruth Chapter 1, Isaiah 6:1

Ruth demonstrates a level of commitment very rarely understood today. Let me tell you a little about commitment and enduring lost coupled with spiritual training. I'm a Vietnam veteran with the Marine Corps. When I returned from Vietnam, I so yearned for a level of camaraderie that I experienced in Vietnam among my fellow marines, but I didn't find anyone in my hometown willing to lay down their lives for me. Then one day I met Jesus Christ, and he told me he was not just willing, but had already "taken a bullet" for me.

I said great, me and this Jesus character understand one another; I can hang with this guy. Then I was told that there was group of Christians that were "Christ like", and I could feel the "old camaraderie" of my fellow marines coming all over me.

Well, needless to say, I'm still looking for the "greater love" that's willing to lay down his life for a friend. When I was in Vietnam, I lost something (blood) when I left Vietnam, I lost something (camaraderie). My lost became a serious spiritual training for me. How do you see it: Trouble or Training?

You choose; because we can do just that, choose!

Legitimate
Opportunity to   **L**egal
See   **OR**   **O**pportunity for
Trouble   **S**piritual
                                Training

LOT

Scripture: Genesis 12:4; 13:8-10

Lot represents a lot; a lot of old mind sets, an attitude that has always gotten man in trouble with His maker. The true challenge in this story started when GOD told Abram to leave family, friends, and familiar circumstances. There was still a promise of offspring and at 75 Abram thought maybe, just maybe, GOD will bring an inheritance through this nephew Lot. Lot had lots of baggage, many issues and "I get it", Abram needed a son and Lot needed a father. The problem is neither one of these were GOD's choice.

Old thinking, I need to help GOD do what He said He was going to do. I think GOD bit off more than He can chew with this one, I need to step in and help him. Sorry Abram, where you are going, not everybody can go with you. GOD took Abram through an advanced course in walking by faith. *Why do you want as an heir, a sight orientated, and money hungry, young man?* It's the old mentality that hinders Abram from receiving all that GOD would have for him.

L.O.T. - Legitimate Old Thinking caused many to die in the wilderness and even made most of Jesus' disciples to stay in the boat, and not have the testimony that they too walked on water.

Legitimate
Old
Thinking

Don't Let It Hinder You!

LOVE

Scripture: John 3:16, John 15:12

This is my commandment, that ye love one another, as I have loved you. But we can't love each other unless we know how GOD loves us. GOD's love is geared toward us bearing fruit, bearing much fruit. But watch out when you bear fruit because afterward comes the cutting, the pruning, so that you and I can bear more fruit, and that our fruit will remain. But if you and I don't bear fruit we'll still be cut, just cut down.

When we love we are:

Leaving

Our

Viciousness

Elsewhere

GOD so loved that He gave…

It's vicious to see someone in need and not give. GOD knew what I needed for redemption, for salvation, for me and my issues and He refused to leave me in the mess that I was in. So, He gave, paid, sacrificed that which was most dear to Him. Verse 12 of **John 15** says,

" There's just no greater love than a man should lay down his life for his friend."

There is no greater love, no comparison to the love that GOD demonstrated through giving his son, Jesus.

MIND

We need to keep our mind free from the opportunity that allows satan to enter in. For as a man thinketh in his heart so is he.

Scripture: Proverbs 23:7, Philippians 4:8

Whatsoever things are true, whatsoever things are honest, whatsoever things are just, whatsoever things are pure…think on these things.

In my mind to think means to put THE/INK to it. As a child in school, I never wanted to use the ink pen, because if you make a mistake, it was harder to erase. So, putting something in ink meant you'd better get it right. It's final.

It is sad to think that GOD is with you, when in fact He is not, and you don't know where He is, nor when you left Him behind?

Think on these things, put them in the ink and allow them to be there permanently, for it's the:

Main

Ingredient

Navigating (our)

Destiny

MOTHER

There are many obstacles to hell that we don't always recognize. A mother's prayers are the main obstacle for preventing her children, and the lives of so many, ending in hell.

Scripture: Exodus 2

Main

Obstacle

To

Hell

Eventually

Recognized

The Hebrew woman conceived and bore a son. In order to preserve his life, she hid him three months. When she could no longer hide him, she made an ark for him. A mother's care for her son is obvious here in this text; so much of what goes on in the mind of mothers can be readily seen in the interaction of animals. Let's look at the mother eagle. She creates a nest for her young, leaves them and goes to get food for them and brings it back to them to eat.

But when she feels it's time for them to fly, she'll take them on her wings and as they hold on for dear life, mama soars into the clouds and then comes down at an alarming speed.

This mother will teach these young eaglets just how to soar and not be comfortable anywhere else except high in the sky where they belong.

Real Mothers know where they want their children to end up, *in heaven not hell*.

PASTOR

"I will give you Pastors according to my heart, who will feed you with knowledge and understanding". They are truly passionate and anointed. They are wired to serve others the truth of the word of GOD. Jesus Christ came to minister and not to be ministered to and Pastors come to serve and not to be served.

Pastors are:

Passionate

Anointed

Servants

Transforming

Our

Relationships

Scripture: Jeremiah 3:15

What a Pastor does is teach, train, and motivate the saints (sheep) in areas of transformation of our relationships with men, women, boys, and girls as well as our relationship with the Heavenly Father.

Another rendering of the word Pastor is Shepherd. We must rid ourselves of a Western mind-set to understand what GOD wants us to know about shepherding. I was in Israel several years ago and had an opportunity to see some shepherds leading sheep and goats across the land. There were two shepherds, one in the front and one in back. One visionary in front and one rear shepherd working to keep the sheep and goats from being scattered. This rear shepherd or assistant pastor looked really rough. The Holy Spirit whispered to me *"You have no right of being up front, until you spent time in the rear"*. Being a Pastor is where we develop the true heart of GOD when we learn to follow.

PEACE

Jesus said "*Peace I leave with you, my peace I give to you, not as the world gives. Let not your heart be troubled, neither let it be afraid.*"

It was a normal day at our place of business "Dora's Loving Childcare". I was holding a little one and was summoned to the phone. The voice on the other end says, *"Are you Charles Kent"?* I said, *"Yes"*. The voice said, "*Your wife has been in a serious car accident*". Thoughts flashed through my mind, thought of everything negative, and all the worst-case scenarios.

I rushed out to the scene of the accident. The police were there, but the ambulance had already taken my wife to the hospital. As I was moving rapidly toward the hospital, GOD spoke these words to me *"I know that you know that I am here*". My response "*oh Lord I know You're here, You're everywhere*". His response, "*Then you need to act like it*".

I slowed down, at least to the speed limit, and made it safely to the hospital where I found my wife in a wheelchair with only minor bruises and scratches.

Scripture: John 14:27

The Holy Spirit reminded me the words of Christ "Peace". Peace is a:

Powerful

Everyday

Awareness (that)

Christ (is)

Everywhere

PLACE

Have you heard a friend say I'm just in a bad place right now? Or maybe you've said this is just a good place for me to be at this time. What are you truly saying? Is it emotional, physical, and spiritual? In my neighborhood we say I'm going to my place; what we mean is where we live, where we sleep, where we eat, where we bathe, etc.

Scripture: John 14:2, Jesus tells His disciple, "*I go to prepare a place for you*". A place, a position; it's filling a void in the Master's absence.

I know sometimes we can feel we're in a bad or a good place. It's how we look at it. Jesus says, "*I am currently occupying your place as the Son of GOD. When I go away there will be a vacancy on earth, a place for you. I must go in order for you to get it.*"

This is my place, my spot, my job, my assignment, my responsibility. GOD asked Adam, *"Where are you?"* Was he speaking physical locale or spiritually? Elijah was hiding under the tree, the question asked was, *"What are you doing here?"* Knowing you're in the right place is a powerful thing.

Jesus said boys I want you to occupy this place. I give you authority on earth, work with it!!

A Place is a:

Powerful

Legacy

After

Christ

Exits or **E**nters

When Jonah was in the big fish's belly, was he in the right place at the right time? It was a place that would propel him into his destiny, it was a good place.

One must, in one's life, make a choice between boredom and suffering --Madame De Stael

44

PLANS

"For I know the plans that I have for you", says the Lord, thoughts of peace and not of evil, to give you a future and a hope.

Scripture: Jeremiah 29:11

Plans that come from GOD are perfect not flawless, but rather mature, complete, thorough. They're legitimate, and not illegitimate they must come from GOD and GOD alone, not a byproduct of someone else's plan for you. The other components of GOD's plan are, they will be anointed, and this word means ability to get the job done. **Isaiah 10:27**; simply says, *"Burdens will be removed, and yokes destroyed because of the anointing"*. There's a system to all of GOD's plans. It would do us well to understand the system that is being used to bring us to our destiny.

GOD's Plans are:

Perfectly

Legitimate

Anointed

Navigation

System

Here's a little question, we know GOD had a plan for Ruth, Naomi, Boaz, Obed, and King David. Ruth was key in marrying Boaz, but what was hindering the mentorship, the relationship, the coaching, and the instructions from Naomi to young Ruth. Was it Ruth's husband? Was it Naomi's husband? Would Ruth and Naomi spend as much time together if both of them had husbands? I know GOD says, *"The plans I have for yo*u", but another version says, *"I know the thoughts I think toward you"*. Remember GOD has a system and it's perfect, it's legitimate, it's anointed, and it will navigate you and me to greatness.

POWER

Luke 4:18 *says, "The spirit of the Lord is upon me, because He has anointed me to preach the gospel to the poor. He has sent me to heal the broken hearted, to proclaim liberty to the captives and recovery of sight to the blind. To set at liberty those who are oppressed."*

"But you shall receive power after that the Holy Ghost has come upon you." **Acts 1:8**

Power means no limits, no boundaries. Much of what GOD wants to get across to us is that He's GOD and has no limits. It's amazing to me how GOD allows challenges to come our way.

Many great men of GOD found themselves in prison, beaten, abused, but the Lord delivered them out of their troubles. In Hebrews in the Hall of Faith many deliverances are mentioned. Then in verse 36 of Chapter 11 it speaks of "others" who had trial of mocking and scourging, yes chains and imprisonment. In verse 37, they were stoned, sawn asunder were tempted, were slain with a sword; they wandered about in sheep skin and goat skin; being destitute, afflicted, tormented; and in verse 38 all these great men of GOD of **whom the world was not worthy of,** died in faith believing. They were prisoners of war but with an evacuation route thereby having P O W E R.

Scripture: Luke 4:18, Acts 1:8, Hebrews 11:36, 38

Power is a:

> **P**risoner
> **O**f
> **W**ar
> **E**vacuation
> **R**oute

PRIDE

Proverbs 16:18 *says, "Pride goes before destruction and a haughty spirit before a fall"*

Scripture: Proverbs 6:17. Proverbs 16:18

King Nebuchadnezzar is the best character to describe pride. This man created a 90-foot-high golden god whom all his subjects were ordered to bow down and worship. One prideful demonstration after another caused his demise.

Pride is a painful ride-- see it for what it truly is—

Pompous
Religious
Ignorance
Destroying
Everything

You can readily see a pompous person with their nose in the air and religious people who are so consistent in their rituals, but ignorant of the righteousness that GOD is looking for.

Let's not live in pride that will destroy everything and everybody that it infects. There are six things that GOD hates, and a proud look is at the top of the list see **Proverbs 6:17**.

PUSH

Rejoice always. Pray without ceasing. In everything give thanks; for this is the will of GOD in Christ Jesus for you.

Scripture: I Thessalonians 5:16-18

We will:

Pray
Until
Something
Happens

A few years ago, I found myself in a country where electricity was not always available. They told me at around midnight the lights might go out, but I shouldn't worry, they would kick on the generator, and it would be ok.

So, as they said, midnight came and no power, but there was also no generator, so it was very dark. I had my iPod, so I decided to just lie still and let my music rock me to sleep. It was very dark and very hot, as I was lying with my arms crossed over my chest. A rather large rodent ran across my arms. I jumped up and franticly tried to locate my suitcase where my weapons were, two cans of 'Off' Insect Repellant. I finally found my weapons of choice and was now armed. If anything moved, I would shoot it, and then decided there's no way would lie down again.

So, the thought came to me to pray, I walked the floor from midnight to dawn, praying with two cans of Off Insect Repellant in my hands. I prayed all night till I saw daybreak. The next night came and at midnight no lights, no generator and no laying down for this brother.

This went on for the ten nights I was stationed on that assignment. I learned how to pray in the dark until I saw the light. True Story!! Pray Until Something Happens, in my case it was daylight.

SEEKING FIRST

In the midst of your problem, GOD will always give you a preview of your promotion. A preview of your dreams brings peace and is a sample of what GOD wants to do in your life.

Scripture: Matthew 6:33 (seek first), 7:5, Revelation 2:4 (first love)

Promotion: There will be plenty and there will be pain. There is a plateau that GOD will take you and other people just cannot go.

In seeking GOD, we have to straighten some things out. When you lose something like keys, you have to straighten up sometime or you will make things even worse, and also make it harder to find that which is lost. If you clean first, then as you are cleaning you may find what you have lost.

Seeking First is:

Searching   **F**orsaking

Eternity   **I**gnorance (and)

Everyday   **R**esisting

Knowing   **S**tupidity

Its   **T**oday

Now

Guaranteed

The first thing to do when you get up each morning is to seek GOD first, and everything else is secondary. If we put GOD first, it not only allows us to keep our life clean but also minimizes the things we may lose.

49

SERVE

If GOD calls you to serve, he has greatness in store for you. If you are not serving GOD, then you will serve something else.

Scripture: Romans 1:9, Psalm 100:2, Acts 13:26

Psalms 100:2 *says "For GOD is my witness, whom I serve with my spirit in the gospel of his Son. Serve the LORD with gladness: come before his presence with singing.* **Acts 13:36,** *David, after he had served his own generation by the will of GOD, fell on sleep…"*

When you serve GOD, you are:

Seriously

Enthusiastic (about)

Receiving

Victory

Everyday

When we serve GOD, we serve HIM with our intellect, which is our mind.

So much is made about being considered as a servant and or serving anyone. It has such a negative connotation that it's a challenge for even those in the body of Christ.

Serving GOD means He's the King and I submit myself to His wishes. What we fail to understand as He is King, He's responsible for everything we need and/or desire. And if we know that, then truly we serve: Seriously Enthusiastically Receiving Victory Every day.

There's a blessing in serving, whether we serve another man or woman of GOD or in the foreign mission field serving those who may never be able to repay you themselves

SLAVE

In our day nobody wants to be labeled a slave. It has such negative connotations, being subjected, mistreated, abused, disrespected, and not enjoying freedom like normal people. In some circle's slaves were not considered as being human beings. Slave masters were seen as gods, one to be adored, looked up to, and esteemed.

But the label put on slaves has always come at the hands of violent men. This is and was the means used to subject people to slavery.

Scripture: John 8:32

The text state, the truth shall set you free, therefore free is the opposite of being a slave. I remember looking this word, Free, up and in the Greek, it means unrestricted, able to move about at will, as a free man and not as a slave. Knowing the truth concerning prosperity prevents us from living in a violent environment, laboring to just find a little peace. Knowledge of the truth concerning healing causes me not to live in sickness and with diseases.

I grew up in some rather violent environments, but never ever did I feel like I was a prisoner to that culture. I was never ever a slave to ignorance. A slave is:

Someone

Laboring (in)

A

Violent

Environment

Nobody holds a good opinion of a man who has a low opinion of himself --Anthony Trollope

SOUND

A sound from heaven, they were all on one accord in one place and suddenly there came a sound from heaven. There were a few things that took place before the "Sound from Heaven" came:

Scripture: Acts 2:1-3

1. They were all on one accord, not just one person but "they" a group of people with one mind
2. They were in one place, with great expectations.

A sound from heaven, it was a word and/or words that GOD used to open and birth the church. This was not the first time this pattern presented itself. In the beginning GOD used a *"Sound from Heaven"* to dismiss the darkness.

In **Genesis 1:1-3**: GOD said, *"Let there be light"* and darkness had to disappear. Abraham and Sarah received a "Sound from Heaven" so when the church got started GOD sent a sound from heaven and I can hear Him say:

SO U Need Direction!!!

GOD knows that, and He has sent a Sound, a Word from Heaven to address our every concern.

The limits of my language means the limits of my world - Ludwig Wittgenstein

STAR

A star only shines in the dark, so when darkness comes in your life, start letting your light shine.

Scripture: Matthew 2:2

"For we have seen His star in the east and have come to worship Him". A Star is someone or something that:

Shows

The

Appropriate

Route (to Jesus)

Add **T** to star and you have **START.**

Shows

The

Appropriate

Route (to Jesus)

Today

Start today showing the appropriate route to Jesus. If you are not showing people how to get to Jesus, then you are not a star and you have not started to shine.

If you are not showing how to get to Jesus you are just rats running around in filth, which is star, spelled backwards.

Real

Aggravating

Time

Spent

STAND

Shadrach, Meshach, and Abednego, answered and said to the King, *"O Nebuchadnezzar, we are not careful to answer thee in this matter, if it be so, our GOD whom we serve is able to deliver us from the burning fiery furnace, and He will deliver us out of thine hand, O King".*

Scripture: Daniel 3: 16-18; 24-25

"But if not, be it known unto thee, O King that we will not serve thy gods, nor worship the golden image which thou hast set up." In other words, we will not bow down to idols.

This story has been told by so many Sunday school teachers over the years. The emphasis has been on the fact that the three Hebrew boys would not bow, they just refused to bow. Well, if they refused to bow then they chose to STAND.

Standing takes tenacity, it takes will power, fortitude, an ability to withstand and stand under the pressure being applied. These boys demonstrated strength with their intolerance to what they saw as nonsense, which was bowing down to idols when they serve the true and living GOD.

They said, *"We will stand, when there's nothing left to do stand."* Many individuals demonstrated this type of tolerance against nonsense, one that comes to mind is Rosa Parks, and she stood by sitting. After you've done what you can, just STAND:

Strong

Tolerance

Against

Nonsense

Daily

54

THIEF

The thief does not come except to steal, kill and destroy.

The thief has a time that he strikes it's never obvious, less his objective is not completed. He gets up early and/or stays up late, with the sole purpose of waiting for you and me to be most vulnerable. He's a hoodlum that'll do whatever it takes to invade any and everybody's future.

Scripture: John 10:10

Please note that a thief only comes for those things that are of value. Therefore, the true determination of the thief is to invade our future. They diminish our plans for a better life by stealing those things dear to us. As it is in the natural, so it is in the spiritual.

How about the word from GOD you and I just heard? Before the day is gone here comes the thief to quickly try to come after those deposits that came from heaven. Your peace and your joy are also things that a thief wants. A thief is a timeless hoodlum infiltrating every body's facilities and future.

My suggestions lock your stuff up; your valuables must be put up and secured in a safe place. My peace must be protected and guarded, my joy you can't take away, and the current word GOD gave me, I will fight to maintain! He comes because we've got goods, precious goods that he wants. We must be ready and watchful. A thief is a:

Timeless

Hoodlum

Invading

Everybody's

Future

TOUCH

Scripture: Matthew 9:20-22

Behold, a woman, which was diseased with an issue of blood 12 years, came behind him and touched the hem of His garment. For she said, *"If I may but touch His garment, I shall be whole"*. Twelve years is a long time to be in need of a healing. This woman shows real tenacity to not give up. So many times, we quit just before the breakthrough. Someone told me long ago you'll feel like a breakdown is around the corner before the breakthrough comes.

There's a cry and persistence going on here. When I was a letter carrier I was introduced to a red Doberman, just a mean demonic animal. I was told they were the meanest animal on the face of the earth. That is until I went to Australia and saw a Tasmanian devil; this ugly creature has the strongest jawbone muscles in all the animal kingdom.

The tenacious persistence of this woman was like that; she pressed her way through the crowd and in her heart said, *"My cry will be dealt with today"*. I will get what I need; I know it's been a long time that I've been crying about this problem, but Jesus is here, and I must touch Him. And there's an Obvious Unique Cry like none other, that gets Jesus's attention and He says, *"Who touched me"*.

A touch like no other, A Unique Cry for Deliverance is:

The

Obvious

Unique

Cry (of)

Hunger

56

TRUTH

Disciples are disciplined followers of Jesus. If you continue in the Word of GOD, you are His disciple. If you continue in His Word, stay in the Word you will know the Truth and the Truth shall make you free.

Scripture: John 8:31

The Strong's concordance defines truth as nothing concealed. When you understand that nothing is concealed, then Jesus has entered your life. The truth is that which is uncovered. When Jesus is on the scene nothing is hidden. The more truth you have the more freedom you have, limited truth, limited freedom. To be free means unrestricted, unrestrained, and able to move about at pleasure.

The   **T**he
   Reality   **R**eal
    Under   **U**nderstanding
   The   **T**oward
    Heavens   **H**eaven

The truth of the matter is based upon your commitment to stay in the word of GOD. GOD will uncover the truth. The more you walk with GOD the more He will reveal to you. GOD wants us to know the truth about ourselves and we need to know His plans, His purpose, and direction for our lives.

Education…has produced a vast population able to read but unable to distinguish what is worth reading --G. M. Trevelyon

TRUST

In order to trust, there must first be respect; we must adore, acknowledge, and understand that GOD is GOD. He was here before there was a beginning. He created time and was in eternality and will forever be.

Understanding spiritual things will require not logic but learning to lean and depend on Jesus Christ. He will defy odds; violate rules just for His children. Change Kings, pull down governments, cause the sun to stand still. We must learn to T. R. U. S. T. There will be trust in our walk with GOD as we trust the word of GOD.

Scripture: II Corinthians 1:21-22, Jeremiah 1:5

Now, *"he which establisheth us with you in Christ: and hath anointed us in GOD."* **II Corinthians 1:21-22**

"Before I formed thee in the belly, I knew thee; and before thou camest forth out of the womb, I sanctified thee." **Jeremiah 1:5**

"How GOD anointed Jesus of Nazareth with the Holy Ghost and with power who went about doing good, and healing all that were oppressed of the devil, for GOD was with him, because he trusted His father." **Acts 10:38**

He that cometh to GOD must believe that He is and Trust that He is:

Trust is:

To

Respect (and)

Understand

Spiritual

Things

WORD

Even Jesus had to deal with the devil; therefore, we should not expect any less. We're sometimes deceived to think our case isn't that bad, I'm not that much of a threat to the enemy; but in all honestly, it's the Word in you that He's most concerned about. Jesus deals with the devil the same way in each temptation. He simply reminds the devil what the Word says. Therefore, simply give the enemy the Word of GOD. It caused Jesus to win over resistance every time. What does the Word say? *"He promised to watch over His Word to perform it."* **Jeremiah 1:12**

Scripture: Matthew 4:3-4, 6-7, 10, Jeremiah 1:12

"If you are the Son of GOD, command that these stones become bread…But He answered and said, it is written, Man shall not live by bread alone, but by every Word that proceeds from the mouth of GOD."

A Word is:

Winning

Over

Resistance

Daily

All you need is, *"***A WORD FITLY SPOKEN** *".*

Words are, of course, the most powerful drug used by mankind
-- Rudyard Kipling

59

YARD

As a child growing up, we had a yard and we were instructed by our parents were to stay in the yard. You can play outside but stay in the yard. Oh yeah! and don't let anybody you don't know in that gate or in the yard.

Scripture: Matthew 22:37

Your
    Area (of)
        Responsibility (and)
        Destiny

When I joined the Marines and found myself in Vietnam, we had a compound/yard with the same instructions. I was familiar with stay within the parameters of the yard. Don't allow anybody to come into the compound.

We had AORs (Areas of Responsibility) and at night while many slept some had to stand "Hole Watch". We were to watch out for the enemy, which would try to get into our compound and/or our yard. No enemy is coming by me while I'm on my watch.

Simply put, *"Not on my Watch"*. In **Matthew 22:37**, Jesus said, *"you shall love the Lord GOD with all your heart, with all your soul, and with your entire mind."* Here lies our responsibility or our yard.

Your area of responsibility (AOR) and destiny depends on you guarding and protecting your heart, your soul, and your mind.

A WORD FITLY SPOKEN FROM DR. CHARLES L. KENT

Let us therefore be zealous and exert into that rest of GOD to know and experience it for ourselves that no one may fall or perish by the same kind of unbelief and disobedience, into which those in the wilderness fell.

When the Word of GOD speaks, according to the Amplified Bible of Hebrews 4:12 it states, "It's alive, operative, energizing, and effective. It is sharper than any two-edged sword, penetrating to the dividing line of the breath of life (soul) immortal spirit, and of the joints and marrow, that is of the deepest parts of our nature. Exposing, sifting, analyzing, and judging the very thoughts and purposes of the heart."

This Word from GOD clearly states that it's the Word of GOD that can divide what is soulish and what is spiritual. The word 'soul' in this passage is the Greek word 'psychē', from which we get the English words psychology and psychiatry, and from where we psychoanalyze the study of the soul.

I believe there can be no understanding of the soul without the word of GOD. It takes the living word of GOD to separate what is of the world and what is of the word of God.

There's no way we can determine what is fleshly, carnal, soulish and what's from heaven, except by and through the word of GOD. It has always been, and in these constant changing times, still the final authority. Jesus said, *"Heaven and earth shall pass away before on jot or tittle of my word shall fail" (Matthew 5:18).*

ABOUT THE AUTHOR
Dr. Charles L. Kent

Born in Chicago, Illinois, but now reside in Arlington, Texas. Dr. Charles Kent is married to the lovely Juleane Kent from Australia. Together they have six children Joshua, Charmaine, Talysa, Courtney, Rebekah, and Isaac. Dr. Kent is also a proud grandfather and great grandfather.

DR. CHARLES KENT

Dr. Charles Kent has over thirty years of working experience in both National and International levels in the areas International Relations and Diplomacy, Global Health and Poverty. As Vice President for Global 2000 (2010) International Accredited Ambassador to the United Nations, an International Humanitarian, Non-Governmental Organization (NGO), he works to promote the aims and objectives of the United Nations and its various agencies Worldwide.

He received a Purple Heart while in the U.S. Marines, for injuries acquired during acts of bravery during his tour of duty in South Vietnam.

Dr. Kent is an avid scholar who has attended various colleges such as Harvard University's John F. Kennedy School of Government. He has a Doctoral Degree in Pastoral Studies and a Master's Degree in Christian Education.

In May 2005, Dr. Kent established a foundation to bring relief to third world countries, called Joseph Outreach Foundation.

Bishop, Pastor Dr. Charles Kent is also an ordained Minister. He holds a position as a board member of Global Apostolic Network, Brisbane, Australia.

Just a Little More on
FAVOR
Faithfulness Appreciated Violating Obvious Rules

Scripture: Deuteronomy 28:2-7

"And all these blessings shall come upon you and overtake you because you obey the voice of the Lord your GOD."

"Blessed shall you be in the city and blessed shall you be in the country. Blessed shall be the fruit of your body, the produce of your ground and the increase of your herds, the increase of your cattle and the offspring of your flocks. Blessed shall be your basket and your kneading bowl. Blessed shall you be when you come in and blessed shall you be when you go out."

Verse #7, *"The Lord will cause your enemies who rise against you to be defeated before your face; they shall come out against you one way and flee before you seven ways."*

The Lord will command the blessing on you in your store houses and to which all you can set your hand …
What a wonderful promise from GOD, so much said there I see a promise as a pro-mission, a positive mission from GOD. It sounds like to me everywhere GOD's people are and go, GOD says we're blessed. Everything we touch, everybody in our camp, our work, EVERYTHING! How can this be when all the rest of the world is not experiencing the same type of blessing?

The Amplified Bible defines blessed as happy, fortunate, one to be envied. Make no mistake it's the favor of GOD obviously on our lives. Faithfulness Appreciated by GOD and therefore GOD decides to violate, break, and circumvent rules for you and me. The truth about Ruth was more than about a kinsman redeemer.

Continued on the Next Page

FAVOR
Faithfulness Appreciated Violating Obvious Rules

There's this subplot of commitment that interest me so, dedication and discipline to someone who cannot be bought. Who isn't in it for the money, and according to scripture these kinds of folk end up getting blessed and walk in favor tremendously.

Ask yourself, How Ruth just "happened" onto Boaz's field? She just happened to be at the right place at the right time to meet the right person. When you're faithful nobody can stop you. GOD will do some strange things just for you and me. Favor ain't fair, you know I know it, and your enemies know it and guess what GOD knows it also.

Have you ever thought about the passage in **Roman 9** where the writer speaks of vessels of honor and dishonor? Vessels of honor are people GOD just decided to show favor to, and yes everything they touch turns to gold. Let's be very clear, favor is from GOD and it's because of faithfulness GOD demonstrates His appreciation. While Joseph was in prison, and in the palace, favor was given to him.

F.A.V.O.R – Faithfulness Appreciated Violating Obvious Rules.

1. Recall how GOD has shown you FAVOR this week, this month or even this year.

   _____
   _____
   _____

2. Have you thanked GOD for his FAVOR on your life?

   _____
   _____
   _____

3. Are you faithful? Realizing faithfulness leads to FAVOR.

   _____
   _____
   _____

Just a Little More on
GIFT
GOD's Instrument For Transformation

Have you heard someone say she's so gifted and makes that look so easy. The truth is it may just be that easy for them and very difficult for the rest of us.

Here's how you know you're gifted and/or talented. When you do what you do (in GOD) and:

1. It blesses you and you enjoy it yourself,
2. It also blesses others and they come to you and say, you really blessed me with that song you sang, or that lesson you taught.
3. You feel a smile from heaven when you do what you do.

You know you are gifted, when you get blessed when you do what you do, and others get blessed when you do what you do, and you sense GOD being blessed when you do what you do.

For Example, I am not a mechanic, never have been, nor have the desire to ever be. I don't care for grease under my fingernails, scratches, and bruises. I don't get excited thinking about breaking a car engine down and putting it back together again. But I have friends who are gifted in that area, they feel GOD when they pick up a wrench, on the other hand I get a headache.

But where I'm gifted, I am truly gifted, and I've learned to stay in my lane. I was in Cape Town, South Africa, I walked in a church on a Friday night about 11pm; the place was a glow with the presence of GOD. On the platform were many young musicians, no one seemed to be over 30 years of age, but the music was like I never heard before.

Continued on the Next Page

GIFT
GOD's Instrument For Transformation

Just as I was so amazed my friend who had brought me there said, "all these young people have no formal training", I could not believe it. The skill, the excellence, the harmony...no way! They were just gifted.

Please understand that with any gift GOD gives He expects it to be used and used to its maximum. Are you doing that or are you burying your gift, talent and or ability? A *G.I.F.T – GOD's Instrument For Transformation.*

1. Have you discovered your GIFT, that special something that GOD has given you?

   _____
   _____
   _____

2. Have you maximized your GIFT?

   _____
   _____
   _____

3. Are you ready for GOD to return and ask you what did you do with I gave you?

   _____
   _____
   _____
   _____
   _____

Just a Little More on
NAME
Now Announcing My Existence

"The invisible things of GOD are clearly seen, being understood by the things that are made." **Romans 1:21**

Let's look at how GOD made things in the book of Genesis. GOD said and He saw, GOD said or spoke things into existence. He was clear on what He wanted, and all creation did not vote, debate, nor dialogue on what GOD said, they obeyed and became whatever GOD said. We marvel at the fact that creation obeys the voice of GOD. Because man is part of GOD's creation, we want to debate on whether what GOD is saying is politically correct.

Is what GOD saying 21st century or is GOD out of date on some points?

GOD gave mankind the image and likeness of Him. Adam (mankind) announced the very existence of the animals, with Father GOD overlooking. What do we call it?

Barren and with no child, "Everybody else has a child except me", Hanna says. "I am just a child", says Jeremiah. "I can't be what you say I can be", and GOD's response is, "Don't say that". I just wonder how many times GOD has said that to you and to me, when we're giving power and/or announcing the very existence of something GOD didn't say.

You say, "I'll never make it through school, I'll never be accepted, and I'll never get a good man or woman". I'll never ever be what GOD wants me to be. GOD is doing a N.E.W. thing and it starts with what is coming out of our mouths. NEW – Never Ever Worked.

Continued on the Next Page

NAME

Now Announcing My Existence

Jesus spoke to the fig tree, spoke to the storms, He had Ezekiel to speak to the dry bones, it's a declaration, a decree, an announcement, debt you have no place in my life.

GOD is mindful of us; He will bless us, both small and great. May the Lord give you increase more and more, you and your children. We came to know Jesus through confessing Him with our mouths and believing Him in our hearts. Everything else we get from GOD will not be by accident we must N.A.M.E it! – Now Announcing My Existence.

Life, Love, Liberty is Mine Today! Wealth and Riches are in my house.

1. Is it a storm or a steppingstone? You C/ALL (see all) it!

    _____
    _____
    _____

2. What is your name? Jacob or Israel, Saul or Paul.

    _____
    _____
    _____

3. You shall have whatsoever you say. True or False. Do you have you what you have been saying?

    _____
    _____
    _____
    _____

68

INDEX

69

INDEX, con't

Additional Testimonies

"Dr. Kent is a master teacher. His passion bursts as he poured into this book. To the casual reader, this book will be impressive because of its sheer size, the book's depth of detail, spiritual jolts, and complexity. It's a book with an inspirational blast for your soul all rolled into one. It is a double-edged sword for the user."

Dr. Melanie P. Manor
Author, "My Bumps Have A Purpose"

"'A Word Fitly Spoken' is exceptionally wonderful stories encapsulating one's mood from childhood to adulthood. This is a snapshot in time we all can relate with a twist to heighten your spiritual senses. Mr. Charles' art of storytelling while providing Bible base resources, scriptures and life experiences deserves high praise. A Word Fitly Spoken shows when you are having *"one of those days"* you have more than just someone, but the comfort of the Heavenly Father and His word."

Thanks
Donna Thomas

"'A Word Fitly Spoken' speaks to those of us that are FIT for the Kingdom of GOD. It is truly for a time such as this."

Min. Dr. Vincent Manor I
Founder – Another Opportunity Sports Inc.

For information and inquiries:

Email: admin@awordfitlyspoken.net
Website: www.awordfitlyspoken.net
Facebook: A Word Fitly Spoken with Dr Charles Kent
You Tube: A Word Fitly Spoken

Please include your testimonies and praise reports
when you write.

www.ingramcontent.com/pod-product-compliance
Lightning Source LLC
LaVergne TN
LVHW051158080426
835508LV00021B/2683